Omnibus Press Presents
the Inside Story of MY
CHEMICAL ROMANCE

Mona Gale

OMNIBUS PRESS

Part of **The Music Sales Group**
New York/London/Paris/Sydney/Copenhagen/Berlin/Tokyo/Madrid

Copyright © Music Sales Corporation
Picture research, cover and book design by Sarah Nesenjuk

ISBN 978-0-8256-7334-4
Order No. OP51832

Exclusive Distributors:
Music Sales Corporation
257 Park Avenue South, New York, NY 10010 USA

Music Sales Limited
14 - 15 Berners St., London W1T 3LJ United Kingdom

Music Sales Pty. Limited
120 Rothschild Street, Rosebery, Sydney, NSW 2018 Australia

Photo Credits:
Front cover © Theo Wargo/WireImage
back cover © Kevin Mazur/WireImage
pg i © Steve Brown/Retna, pg iii © Tina Korhonen, pg iv © Eddie Malluk/WireImage, pg vi © Kevin Mazur/WireImage, pg 2 © Steve Trager/Frank White Photo Agency, pg 4 © Justin Borucki/Retna, pg 6 © Sam Newman/WireImage, pg 7 © Frank White/Frank White Photo Agency, pg 8 © Anthony Saint James/Retna Ltd, pg 10 © Eddie Malluk/WireImage, pg 12 © Steve Trager/Frank White Photo Agency, pg 13 © Frank White/Frank White Photo Agency, pg 14 © Theo Wargo/WireImage, pg 17 © Steve Trager/Frank White Photo Agency, pg 18 © Steve Trager/Frank White Photo Agency, pg 20, 23 © Kelly A. Swift/Retna, pg 24 © Theo Wargo/WireImage, pg 26 © Eddie Malluk/WireImage, pg 28 © Jamie McCarthy/WireImage, pg 31 © Theo Wargo/WireImage, pg 32 © Lester Cohen/WireImage, pg 33 © Justin Borucki/Retna, pg 34 © Steve Trager/Frank White Photo Agency, pg 36 © Kevin Kane/WireImage, pg 38 © Jamie McCarthy/WireImage, pg 40 © Rowen Lawrence/WireImage , pg 43 © Peter Doherty/Retna, pg 44 lft © Frank White/Frank White Photo Agency, pg 44 rt © Scarlet Page, pg 45 © Vicki Berliner/Retna UK, pg 45 rt © Steve Trager/Frank White Photo Agency, pg 46 © Justin Borucki/Retna, pg 47 © Jeffrey Mayer/WireImage, pg 48 © Justin Borucki/Retna, pg 48 top rt © Frank White/Frank White Photo Agency, pg 49 btm rt © Justin Borucki/Retna, pg 49 © Andy Stubbs/WireImage, pg 50 © Robb D. Cohen/Retna LTD, pg 51 © Eddie Malluk/WireImage, pg 53 © James Sharrock/WireImage, pg 54 © Jeffrey Mayer/WireImage, pg 56 © Eddie Malluk/WireImage, pg 57 © Barry Brecheisen/WireImage, pg 58 © Bill McCay/WireImage, pg 60 © John Shearer/WireImage, pg 61 © John McMurtrie/Retna UK, pg 62 © John Shearer/WireImage, pg 65 © Theo Wargo/WireImage, pg 67 © Kevin Kane/WireImage, pg 68 © Gene Ambo / Retna, pg 70 © Sam Newman/WireImage, pg 72 © Theo Wargo/WireImage, pg 73 © Sam Newman/WireImage, pg 74 © Sam Newman/WireImage, pg 76 © Theo Wargo/WireImage, pg 78 © Peter Doherty/Retna, pg 81 © Frank White/Frank White Photo Agency, pg 82 © Barry Brecheisen/WireImage

Printed in the Unites States of America
Visit Omnibus Press at www.omnibuspress.com

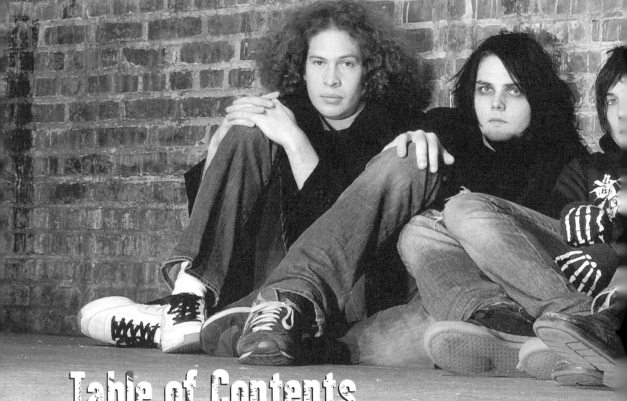

Table of Contents

My Chemical
Romance

Mike
Jones

Chapter 1

JERSEY PUNKS

New Jersey may lay claim to the title of "Garden State," but it was far from an idyllic setting for Gerard and Mikey Way, pivotal members of My Chemical Romance, as they grew up in the tough Essex County neighborhood of Belleville. Sandwiched between rough-and-tumble Paterson and Newark, Belleville is home to about 35,000 working-class people. Despite the best efforts of local law enforcement, burglaries, car theft, and assaults plagued the town during the Way brothers' childhoods. It was so bad that they opted to spend most of their time safely ensconced in their home reading comic books, watching cartoons, and playing Dungeons & Dragons. Mikey once told *Alternative Press* that, "Our parents were kind of scared to let us outside of the house, because where we lived was pretty dangerous." Gerard agreed, "Me and Mikey couldn't really play where we grew up, which was pretty much the same story with everybody, because it was so f***ing dangerous. We had to construct our own world which we lived in constantly."

Older brother Gerard was born on April 9, 1977 in Newark to parents of Italian and Scottish descent. Way's dad Donald is a service manager at a Bloomfield car dealership and his mom Donna was formerly a hairdresser. Always interested in music, Gerard scored the lead part in a fourth-grade production of *Peter Pan*. His parents and grandmother Elena—who encouraged him to become a graphic artist and musician—beamed with pride, but they never guessed how much time Gerard and Mikey would end up spending on stage in the future. As a teenager, Gerard worked as a bagger in a grocery store and a clerk in a comic book store and happily graduated high school in 1995. From there, he attended the School of Visual Arts in New York City. He got his diploma in 1999 with dreams of becoming a cartoon animator.

Mikey, just a few years younger than Gerard, was born in Newark on September 10, 1980 as Michael James Way. He enjoyed an uneventful childhood and didn't really have a clear picture of what he wanted to do with his life when he graduated from high school. He worked at a Barnes & Noble bookstore for a while (and even got Gerard a job there too), interned for Eyeball Records (which would turn out to be very fortuitous), and went to college part-time before finally dropping out.

The brothers Way lived in their own world while attending high school, mainly playing the part of outcasts and geeks. It's safe to say none of their classmates ever considered the two would end up in one of punk rock's most incendiary bands. Here is their story.

Chapter 2
AftER 9/11, a BAnD is bOrN

In early 2000, you could find Gerard marking time in Jersey and New York City and feeling more than a tad pathetic because he still lived in the basement of his mom's house. He was trying to sell a cartoon concept called *Breakfast Money* to the Cartoon Network where he happened to be interning at the time. The star of the show was an endearing simian that possessed the odd ability to magic-up any imaginable breakfast food at any time.

Unfortunately, the network turned the show down because they already had *Aqua Teen Hunger Force* in production, a show that was coincidently also about food.

"Something just clicked in my head that morning. i literally said to myself, 'F*** art. i've gotta get out of the basement. i've gotta see the world. i've gotta make a difference!" –Gerard

Gerard slipped into depression as he saw his life at a standstill. Then, the horrific events of the September 11, 2001 terrorist attacks happened. After viewing the fall of the Twin Towers in Manhattan while on the clock for the Cartoon Network, he knew he had to change his life. He was miserable and felt like he was heading nowhere. Things had to change.

Talking to *Spin* about his reaction to 9/11 in the September 25, 2005 issue, Gerard admitted, "Something just clicked in my head that morning. I literally said to myself,

'F*** art. I've gotta get out of the basement. I've gotta see the world. I've gotta make a difference!" From that moment on, he thought of one thing: Forming a band and playing the music he loved—emo and goth-punk—for a living.

Gerard had always loved music and his early influences were the New Jersey-based band The Misfits, Black Flag, Morrissey, At The Gates, Descendents, Pantera, The Cure, and The Smiths.

Iron Maiden was also important in Way's musical development: "Well it started really young with Bruce Dickinson [Iron Maiden]. He really inspired me 'cause he's a great front man, a great singer, and I've always been influenced by the way he sang," Gerard told *MetalUnderground.com* in June 2004. "Also, obviously, Geoff [Rickly] from Thursday [another New Jersey band] inspired me as a person to just get up and do that. I've been a fan of music and I've always wanted to be in a band. I just never had the urge to be a front man until I saw him do it. I was like, 'You know what? It just seems so incredible and it seems like he's actually making a difference and he was doing something.' Right at that moment is when I knew I would do it."

With inspiration coming from bands like Iron Maiden, you may think that Gerard was predisposed to go the hard rock/heavy-metal route. Instead, he was drawn to the aggressive emo/punk-rock movement. Here was an outlet for all his angst. He could yell and scream and kick while saying something intelligent about the world and his feelings. He dreamed of a band that could have a hard-driving edge and play pop-punk with a bit of goth thrown in for good measure. He loved what Morrissey did with his music...pairing unhappy lyrics with upbeat music. In the *Life On The Murder Scene* DVD, Gerard explained the appeal of Morrissey's music, "How bleak it was in contrast to how pop it was." Gerard felt that was a key component that lead to Morrissey's success.

In late 2001, Gerard started building the core of what would become My Chemical Romance. "I ran into [drummer] Matt [Pelissier] at a bar and said, 'You know what? I've been writing songs. You're not doing anything, and I'm not doing anything, so let's get together and give it a shot,'" he told the *Alternative Press*.

The pair started writing songs together and eventually came up with the 9/11-inspired "Skylines And Turnstiles" based on Gerard's experience of seeing the Twin Towers crumble. The vibe was positive and both felt they were on to something. At that point they invited lead guitarist Ray Toro to join the band. "I said the same thing I had said to Matt: No strings attached; you don't have to say yes or no," Gerard continued.

> "My dad played drums and my grandfather played drums in bands, so i was always around music."
>
> -Frank

"Just come, check it out, and bring your guitar."

Like the Ways and Matt, Ray also grew up in New Jersey, in Kearny near the Harrison border. Born as Ray Toro Ortiz on July 15, 1977, he had exactly one interest: playing guitar. He attended Kearny High School and spent his time revering the music and playing styles of Iron Maiden, Randy Rhoads, Stevie Ray Vaughan, Slash, Jimi Hendrix, Kirk Hammett of Metallica, and Jimmy Page.

After refining several songs, the trio decided to record a demo in Matt's attic. Fans affectionately call the results the "Attic Demos." "My attic had no walls. It was a wooden, run-down piece of crap. I had a really cheap 16-track board, and we had a bunch of crappy mics," Matt told the *Alternative Press*. "I basically had the drums and guitars playing upstairs and ran mics down the stairs and had Gerard sing in the bathroom." The tracks recorded eventually became "Our Lady Of Sorrows" (originally dubbed "Bring More Knives"), "Cubicles," and "Skylines And Turnstiles."

"You could hear that it was something really new, and it was kind of a weird idea, but for some reason, as poorly as it was coming together, it really worked. And a lot of people loved the demo," Gerard told the *Alternative Press*.

With several demo tracks under their belts, the band had to get serious and finalize the lineup. They did so by enlisting Gerard's brother Mikey to play bass and drafting another Jersey-ite, Frank Iero, to play rhythm guitar. Gigs around the state and the Northeast started trickling in. First they played basements parties and finally graduated to local clubs like the Loop Lounge in Passaic and the Bloomfield Ave. Café & Stage in Montclair.

Born on Halloween 1981, Frank Anthony Iero grew up in Belleville. He was the product of a broken home and saw first-hand how difficult it can be for a family to make ends meet. According to Frank, "My parents split up when I was pretty young, my mom was kind of left to take care of everything. There were times when we really couldn't even afford milk." Still, he has a deep love for his hometown and New Jersey in general. "I don't know if it's because I don't see home anymore or I'll never change my opinion on it. I wouldn't change my upbringing for the world," he said.

Iero's musical gift comes naturally. Both his father and grandfather were musicians. "My dad played drums and my grandfather played drums in bands, so I was always around music," Frank told Darin Longman of *University Wire* in May 2005. "I remember growing up and listening to them talk about gigs they were in or places they had played."

As for other musical influences, Iero "was never much for cock rock virtuoso guitar players. I like metal, but it wasn't something that I was inspired to play. I wanted to be Thurston Moore [Sonic Youth]. I wanted to be a normal guy who put his emotions through a guitar."

It was actually Mikey that came up with the name My Chemical Romance. While working at Barnes & Noble, he was inspired by the book *Ecstasy: Three Tales of Chemical Romance* by author Irvine Welsh (who also penned *Trainspotting*).

Bestselling Ecstasy told a trio of stories: A paralyzed romance writer tries to exact revenge on her unfaithful husband, a couple try to cripple a man who marketed Thalidomide (the drug that crippled her), and two Edinburgh slackers meet in a club and explore drugs and house music. It's a compelling read for sure and all members of the band were immediately smitten by the moniker.

Frank was attending Rutgers University on a scholarship when he joined My Chemical Romance, but he eventually dropped out. College was irrelevant at that point. No stranger to playing live, Frank had previously done a stint in the Eyeball Records band Pencey Prep before they dissolved. He also played with Hybrid, Sector 12, I Am a Graveyard, and briefly with Give Up The Ghost.

Frank also counts the Beastie Boys, Black Flag, The Bouncing Souls, and American Nightmare among his influences. Perhaps because he suffered from so many illnesses as a child—including Epstein-Barr virus, bronchitis, and ear infections—Frank grew up with a definite "underdog" complex. That makes him fit right in with My Chem! He thrived on the band's energy and helped make their early appearances a success.

"There is nothing that can compare to the energy that you get when you are playing at the same level as kids... it is just a wall of energy that is conjured up, and it is this really magical thing that happens. Those were some of the best times in the band's life." –Ray

With the band lineup firmly in place and gigs galore, the quintet began the arduous task of building a fan base. And, to everyone's surprise, it wasn't that hard. Playing scores of basement parties made a huge impact on Jersey locals. "It was a crazy, crazy time," Ray told Catherine Holahan of the *Bergen Record* in October 2005. "There is nothing that can compare to the energy that you get when you are playing at the same level as kids... It is just a wall of energy that is conjured up, and it is this really magical thing that happens. Those were some of the best times in the band's life. Now we play on stages that have barricades, and those shows are great, but there is no comparison to [the Jersey shows]. You're in a basement, so you can't move, but you get so excited that you want to jump...It's insane."

During this time period, My Chem shared a rehearsal space with bands Pencey Prep and Thursday. According to Mikey, the bands "would practice in the same room, which was great because you could just hang out and watch someone else's practice, do your own, share ideas, show people what was going on. It was awesome!"

The guys truly found a sense of purpose in each other and their newly formed band: "We didn't like where we were and what we'd become," Gerard told Gene Stout, pop music critic of the *Seattle Post-Intelligencer*. "So we were trying to fulfill some sort of destiny. We felt something calling us. We thought, 'Let's start a band.'"

Chapter 3

Leaving the bASeMENT bEhinD

What you have to understand about New Jersey is that in the late Nineties and early 2000s, it was as important to the punk revival movement as Seattle was to grunge and Athens, Georgia was to Eighties new wave. It was the place to be and My Chemical Romance came up at an opportune time when fans were rabid and record labels were searching for the next big thing.

"It's the most unique scene in the world," Gerard told Tammy La Gorce of the *New York Times* on August 14, 2005. "I look at it now in a very nostalgic way. I definitely miss it. This state is a mecca for music, but where we're

"We always had a vision but we weren't sure if it would translate or just come off as pretentious." -Mikey

from is a lot different than most Jersey bands, and it's important to recognize that about us. This neighborhood [Belleville] is not an area with money. It was very dangerous growing up here. I think that's why we're so into horror movies. It was too scary to play outside as a kid."

So Jersey was beginning to spin out some hardcore punk bands and the nation was finally taking notice. All the while, My Chemical Romance continued to write songs, play basements and clubs, and plan their next move.

It was the late 1990s and the band took any gig they could get. They needed to build a following and get used to performing in front of a crowd. During this time period, a lot of bands played house parties. Geoff Rickly, lead singer of Thursday, threw many such events for the punkerati during those years. My Chem got to know his basement very well. Gerard told the *New York Times*, those get-togethers were "a way to keep the focus on music, instead of going to bars where kids couldn't get in anyway and people were only interested in getting bombed."

Alex Saavedra, industry insider and owner of Eyeball Records, signed many of the bands that played Rickly's basement, including Geoff's own band Thursday, My Chemical Romance, and Midtown. "You could fit maybe 100 people in there," Alex recalled, "and then you'd have kids in the driveway, in the backyard, kids with their ears pressed against the windows trying to listen. It was the sweatiest, smelliest thing, but it was incredible." Geoff concurred: "It was a little sanctuary of a place. So many kids would show up that we'd open the storm windows so they could hear. One time we flagged down an ice cream truck for 300 kids."

While playing the "basement" circuit, Mikey was interning at Eyeball Records. It gave the band the perfect opportunity to hang out with Alex Saavedra. He was a fixture in the New Jersey music scene, as was Mikey. The younger Way brother would do whatever was needed for the label, from papering neighborhoods with flyers for shows, to administrative work, to schlepping equipment for different bands. Alex took notice of Mikey and started inviting him to parties. These events were legendary in

Jersey where musicians, record execs, and fans often ended up at Alex's house partying all night.

"Sometimes the parties were totally impromptu," explained Geoff Rickly to the *Alternative Press*. "It was just a bunch of guys at the house getting drunk, having fun, getting arrested, and having to go to jail. Then there were these huge parties Alex would throw that would be a few hundred people at the house. Half the Jersey scene would be there. It would be everyone from the kids who'd go to the shows to a lot of the bands to everyone who ran the clubs."

Mikey eventually introduced Gerard to Geoff who asked him to draw some T-shirt designs for Thursday. "I was this hermit artist kid who was Mikey's weird older brother," recalled Gerard to the *Alternative Press*. "I met Geoff outside of a record store called St. Marks in Kearny, and I remember this really strange-looking kid who looked like he was in Joy Division. He had a black mop; he looked emaciated and pale-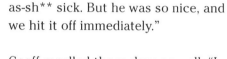as-sh** sick. But he was so nice, and we hit it off immediately."

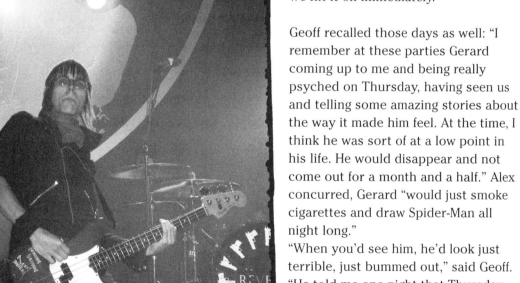

Geoff recalled those days as well: "I remember at these parties Gerard coming up to me and being really psyched on Thursday, having seen us and telling some amazing stories about the way it made him feel. At the time, I think he was sort of at a low point in his life. He would disappear and not come out for a month and a half." Alex concurred, Gerard "would just smoke cigarettes and draw Spider-Man all night long."

"When you'd see him, he'd look just terrible, just bummed out," said Geoff. "He told me one night that Thursday gave him new hope and he was gonna start a band with his little brother. Not that it was a joke, but I thought, yeah, they're thinking about starting a band, but how long does it take you before you actually start doing something good? He would sit there and play me songs on one of Alex's guitars that was so hopelessly out of tune and broken with bad strings that I couldn't even tell what he was doing. But I was like, I love you and your brother, and sure, man; I'll hang out. I'll come to practice.'"

As My Chem got more heavily involved in the Jersey scene, all the right people began to take notice. Mikey also finally got up the nerve to play Alex Saavedra their demo tape during one of his infamous parties. A deal was struck then and there. The band hunkered down and made a commitment to rehearse and write songs and show the kids of New Jersey just how good emo could be.

"We always had a vision," Mikey told *Spin* magazine, "but we weren't sure if it would translate or just come off as pretentious. We were playing basements and Gerard would be like straight-up Ziggy Stardust. Kids would be horrified."

Chapter 4
BULLetS BReAKThRough

With a record deal safely tucked in their collective back pocket, the band got down to brass tacks early in 2002 to record their debut album, *I Brought You My Bullets, You Brought Me Your Love*. Eyeball Records set them up in a New Windsor, N.Y., facility called Nada Studios. While this is the place many up-and-coming bands now come to record demos, EPs, and full-length records, it wasn't even a real studio when My Chem recorded their debut. In fact, owner and chief engineer John Naclerio was still working out of his mother's basement that he outfitted with a Pro Tools system. He recorded *Bullets* and has reaped the benefits ever since. Now, even more bands want to record at Nada with John after seeing the success of My Chem's first album. The band also invited Geoff Rickly, lead singer of Thursday, to produce the record. With the core team in place, the band went full blast into production.

The sessions weren't always smooth, however. Emotions ran high. This was My Chem's big chance and the pressure was mounting. It was also the band's first time recording with a professional engineer and there was a certain learning curve for everyone involved. It didn't help that mother nature got in the way by throwing down an intense storm just as Gerard was psyching himself up to sing some lead tracks. According to Alex in an *Alternative Press* interview, "As soon as it came time for Gerard to do vocals for 'Vampires,' this insane storm hit. Gerard was getting very frustrated because it was his first time recording, decently, in an actual studio. He was overwhelmed and he was over-thinking it...So I punched him in the face!" That's one way to trigger someone's reset button! "I remember it hurting a lot," said Gerard, "and going, 'All right, I hope I can do this.' I remember singing, and something clicked. I remember Alex's face was just amazed that the song was finally coming together. I think it was the second take that we ended up using."

Alex's unorthodox technique worked and Gerard's vocal performances on this album are stellar. His voice is fiery and passionate but there's a good amount of self-reflection thrown in for good measure. Between My Chem's lyrics and Gerard's vocal inflection, it's no wonder so many people react strongly to this music...it speaks to fans on a very deep level.

On July 23, 2002, Eyeball Records released My Chem's debut album. Songs included: "Honey, This Mirror Isn't Big Enough For The Two Of Us" / "Vampires Will Never Hurt You" / "Drowning Lessons" / "Our Lady Of Sorrows" / "Headfirst For Halos" /

Brian Schechter Takes On My Chem

In the middle of August 2002, a tour manager by the name of Brian Schechter caught My Chem's live show at Maxwell's in Hoboken, N.J. He immediately saw the band's potential and began talking with the guys about representing them full-time. This was the band Brian would give up the road for. This was the band he'd invest his life savings in to promote. He knew My Chemical Romance was going to make an impact on the international music scene. However, My Chem was careful about letting someone new into the fold. Brian wouldn't secure a deal with the band until February 17, 2003. The first thing Brian did was put the band on tour with The Used.

"Skylines And Turnstiles" / "Early Sunsets Over Monroeville" / "This Is The Best Day Ever" / "Cubicles" / "Demolition Lovers" / "Vampires Will Never Hurt You" (bonus video) / and "Honey This Mirror Isn't Big Enough For The Two Of Us" (bonus video). When the reviews started coming in, the band was flattered and annoyed to read so many comparisons to New Jersey compatriots, Thursday. It was a foregone conclusion that comparisons would be made. After all, both bands embrace emo, both are from New Jersey, both were signed to Eyeball Records, and Thursday's lead singer Geoff Rickly produced their album!

Alex Henderson reviewed the album for *All Music Guide* saying, *"I Brought You My*

Bullets, You Brought Me Your Love is a generally decent effort—one that deals with a lot of negative emotions and does so in a very candid way. Some will find the lyrics depressing, but then, rock music isn't obligated to press the smile button 24 hours a day. Sadness, pessimism, anger, disillusionment—none of which are difficult to find on this album—are, like happiness, pleasure, and optimism, valid areas of rock expression. *I Brought You My Bullets, You Brought Me Your Love* falls short of exceptional, but it's a noteworthy, generally respectable debut for the New Jersey combo."

Henderson, like other journalists, noted that while My Chem's music is akin to an aggressive, shout-out, their lyrics are actually quite introspective. This quality alone puts them in the category of Nirvana, Blink-182, and Creed. Their music may be dark, but it also encourages listeners to dig deeper into their psyche and figure out who they truly are and what they believe.

Not everyone immediately fell in love with these Jersey-ites though, Stephan Haag of *PopMatters.com* wrote in his album review, "The lesson that I hope My Chemical Romance learn from their debut album is this: Doom 'n' gloom rock, when properly executed, requires a level of theatricality (again, see A.F.I.), which MCR simply haven't attained. The lyrics wouldn't be half as ridiculous if they were delivered with the appropriate goth bravado. My Chemical Romance haven't made the goth varsity team yet."

The lyrics Haag may have been referring to are:

"The amount of pills I'm taking counteracts the booze I'm drinking" from "Honey, This Mirror Isn't Big Enough For The Two Of Us" and "I Think I'll Love to Die Alone" from "Cubicles."

Okay, so the album is a tad melancholy and maybe the guys seem disillusioned and pessimistic about life, but these songs rock! You'd have to be deaf not to hear the blood-pumping rhythms cast out by drummer Matt and guitarists Ray and Frank.

With the album getting reviews—some good, some bad—and local radio airplay, the band continued to play live every chance they got and build their fan base. Bigger things were on the horizon.

Chapter 5
GOOdbYE iNDie; hELlo REPRiSe

2003 ushered in the year of "emo." Even the *New York Times* took notice of the trend and began covering this genre of "tender" punk rock. As the industry woke up to the change in the musical landscape, major labels started signing emo, goth, and punk bands like there was no tomorrow. New Jersey bands were especially sought after. It was a foregone conclusion then that My Chem would be snatched up by a major and lose their indie status. Craig Aaronson, A&R executive for Reprise (part of Warner Bros.) won the band over and signed them in 2003. By the summer, the major labels were trying to turn emo into the next mainstream phenomenon and My Chemical Romance was part of the first wave assault.

At the end of April, the band played the third annual Skate and Surf Festival at Asbury Park Convention Hall in New Jersey. With a capacity of just 5,000, My Chem played with three dozen other bands including Onelinedrawing, Thrice, Armor For Sleep, and The Used. They opened their set with "Honey, This Mirror Isn't Big Enough For The Two Of Us."

The rest of the year was pretty much spent on the road as the band tried to cement their place as the darlings of emo/goth punk. The pace was frantic and the stress was taking its toll on the entire band, especially Gerard who was drinking and taking various drugs like Xanax, which is generally prescribed to ease anxiety and instills a "devil may care" attitude among those abusing it. But My Chemical Romance was determined to make it, no matter what the cost.

When they finally took a break from touring, the band was ready to record their follow-up album, *Three Cheers For Sweet Revenge*. This would be their first major-label album and Reprise entrusted producer Howard Benson to take My Chem to the next level. Howard is known for producing crystalline vocal tracks and has worked with Papa Roach, P.O.D., Hoobastank, and The All-American Rejects.

"We always felt we were much more of a rock 'n' roll band." –Gerard

Since the record was made out in California, the boys had to temporarily relocate: "We actually drove to Los Angeles with all our stuff, and we lived in these apartments called the Oakwood Apartments," Gerard told MTV. "Oakwood is basically home to child actors, out-of-work bands, and porn stars. We saw a lot of child actors hanging out by the pool, constantly drinking. They were like 15 years old, wasted and having these crazy Hollywood parties."

A lot was at stake with this album. Reprise took a chance on them but if this album flopped, they'd be back to playing house parties in a New York minute. They knew they had to work harder than ever and stretch the boundaries of their musical approach. "We took a lot of risks on this record because we knew we had been put into the genre of emo because of the tours we were doing," Gerard told MTV. "We always felt we were much more of a rock 'n' roll band. So that's what we really tried to assert this time." Howard Benson also pushed the band to work harder on song structure and it paid off. *Revenge* as a whole is a stronger album than *Bullets*.

"All of us grew up as geeks, getting picked on and being told we weren't good enough. it's not meant to inspire you to acts of violence. Everything is a metaphor." -Gerard

Revenge is conceptual in nature and the songs tell the story of a couple: "We had a song called 'Demolition Lovers,' from our first record," Gerard told MTV. "In the end of that, the main character and his girlfriend get gunned down in the desert. So, on this album, he's in hell looking for her, and the devil tells him she's still alive. And he says, 'I have to be with her,' and the devil says, 'Then bring me the souls of 1,000 evil men. I'll send you back to earth, and when you kill the last one, you'll find her.'" How romantic.

Gerard explained his line of thinking in a *New York Times* interview: "*Three Cheers* is a concept album about a man who comes back from the dead to kill people who shut him out for not fitting in during his lifetime. The band lent itself to that sort of thing. All of us grew up as geeks, getting picked on and being told we weren't good enough. It's not meant to inspire you to acts of violence. Everything is a metaphor."

The album certainly revolved on many levels. The Way brothers had recently lost their grandmother. They missed out on the last few months of her life because of their frenetic touring schedule. This loss affected both brothers but was particularly devastating to Gerard. "There is a pseudo-concept," revealed Gerard to *Rolling Stone*. "But really it's about two boys living in New Jersey who lost their grandma, and how their brothers in the band helped them get through it."

The record was very personal for this close-knit band. "It always felt to us like this band is about fulfilling a destiny," Gerard explained to MTV. "And the story of the record is linked to that. There's this guy who's doing very much what he feels he should be doing and if he has to kill 1,000 evil men to get to the woman he loves, then he'll do it. And there's a lot of sacrifices we make as well."

Vivid vocal performances are the hallmark of this record. To encourage the intimacy needed to sing these songs, producer Howard Benson locked Gerard in the attic of the studio so he could capture the singer's screams sans any twinges of self-consciousness. "No one was allowed in there when I was doing my thing," Gerard recalled to MTV. "At first it was weird because I'm a showoff and I like people being able to watch me when I'm in the booth. But now, I can't imagine doing it any other way. I really let some intense stuff come out because I became very comfortable being naked and alone like that."

Gerard further exposed himself by creating the watercolor image used as the cover for the album. It's a stunning image of a man and a woman spattered with blood, presumably their own.

On June 8, 2004, Reprise released *Three Cheers For Sweet Revenge* with tracks "Helena" / "Give 'Em Hell, Kid" / "To The End" / "You Know What They Do To Guys Like Us In Prison" / "I'm Not Okay (I Promise)" / "The Ghost Of You" / "The Jetset Life Is Gonna Kill You" / "Interlude" / "Thank You For The Venom" / "Hang 'Em High" / "It's Not A Fashion Statement, It's A Deathwish" / "Cemetery Drive" / and "I Never Told You What I Do For A Living."

The instant the record was released, fans knew it was something special. This was confirmed when the album hit #1 on *Billboard's* Heatseeker chart. It assaulted other charts too, peaking at #28 on *Billboard's* 200 Album chart and #103 on the Top Internet Album chart.

The singles that got the most attention were "I'm Not Okay (I Promise)," "Helena," and "The Ghost Of You." Each went into heavy rotation on radio and on MTV. The first single was "I'm Not Okay (I Promise)." Gerard told MTV at the time, "I like to think of it as a cry for help trapped in a pop song. When I was writing it, I was remembering how hard it was to be a 16-year-old in high school. I always wanted to be an artist, so I was this loner kid who just got drunk all the time. I only had one real friend." He went on to tell MTV why he thought this song was important in the larger scheme of things, "There was a girl I really liked, and she ended up taking really sleazy photographs with her boyfriend, and that really crushed me. I was just swimming in this pit of despair, jealousy, and alcoholism. And when someone's in that situation, it's very rare that they turn to their mom or their best friend and say, 'Hey, I'm not OK. I'm in really bad shape.'" Fans the world over can relate to this type of depression and the song has been an outlet for many people suffering from various disappointments in their lives.

The song peaked at #4 on *Billboard's* Modern Rock Tracks chart, #64 on the Pop 100, and #86 on the Hot 100.

Riding such a high, the band decided to film a video for "I'm Not Okay (I Promise)" which they posted to their *MySpace.com* Web site before sending it off for rotation on MTV.

"Marc Webb [director] came up with this idea to make a fake movie and have the video be the trailer for the fake movie," Gerard told MTV. "I love it. He put us in prep school. The school from *Donnie Darko* is in it. The whole thing feels like *Rushmore*. The first time we all saw it on TV, we sh** ourselves."

The next single and video released was the ultra-personal "Helena," which was a tribute to Elena Lee Rush. Elena—Gerard and Mikey's grandmother—had passed away in 2003. This event haunted Gerard and this song is the outcome of his angst about not getting to say goodbye. *Rolling Stone* printed Gerard's take that the song "is an angry open letter to myself for being on the road so long and missing the last year of

her life." He went even further about his self-hate by telling the *New York Times* that it's "about the situation I've put us in. We're away from home so much, everybody misses their loved ones. I feel very responsible." This sort of guilt and responsibility triggered a lot of Gerard's drug and alcohol abuse around this time period.
While writing the song, Gerard felt it might be something special, telling *Spin*, "I did have some sense it was going to be huge, but it almost had to be to honor a woman so amazing. When she died, I told her we would make a record so f***ing loud that she would hear it all the way in heaven...or wherever it is you go. I was worried about it being huge because it was so personal—I didn't want to exploit my pain and her death."

"Helena" peaked at #13 on *Billboard's* Hot Digital Songs chart, #11 on the Modern Rock Tracks chart, #31 on the Pop 100, and #33 on the Hot 100.

For the video, they once again called upon director Marc Webb. The concept focuses on the funeral of a young girl at which the band members are the pallbearers. The mourners are actual My Chem fans that signed up to be video extras at the band's Web site. An extended interpretive dance segment sets this video apart from others. At the time, Gerard told MTV, "When I first read the treatment for the new video, I got emotional. I realized it was going to be very sad. The song is about my grandmother, who passed away. She taught me how to sing and paint and how to perform. She was an artist, and she pushed me to be an artist. We were really close, so making the video was really good closure for me, personally. It's one of those things where I knew I was going to have to face my fears."

There was more at work during the filming of "Helena." Besides being a watershed moment for Gerard, the band knew it could put them on the creative map. "There's pressure," Gerard admitted to MTV, "but we know that the video for 'Helena' is our chance to be known as a 'video' band. We could be like the Smashing Pumpkins, a band that always made these movies instead of just a bunch of guys in a basement. I think it's going to be very different from 'I'm Not Okay.' It's not funny at all. The best way to describe the video is very sad and celebratory, upsetting and uplifting at the same time. It was a risk, but we've always taken risks. And this video is the biggest risk we've ever taken."

"The choreographer [Michael Rooney] who worked on Bjork's 'It's Oh So Quiet' video worked on this one. It's a funeral, so it's very somber and very depressing, but as soon as the fast part of the song kicks in, everybody starts dancing in this Busby Berkeley style," Gerard told MTV. "And the girl in the coffin [actress Tracey Phillps] dances, and it's really beautiful. When I watched it through the monitor I got so upset I had to leave the room. It's really sad. Because it's her last dance."

Gerard continued, "Marc was very respectful about the whole thing. He was very careful about [the scene where] the girl comes out of the coffin. He thought that would be in bad taste, especially since there were so many things in the video that resembled real life. Marc and I and the art directors didn't really talk too much about what it was going to look like. And then we showed up and the coffin was the same, the church was very similar. Everything was pretty much the same as my grandmother's funeral, so that was pretty heavy."

With two breathtaking videos behind them, My Chem soon became the new favorites of MTV's *Total Request Live* show. In fact, "I'm Not Okay" and "Helena" quickly became heavy rotators on *TRL*.

The third single release was "The Ghost Of You" and it peaked at #38 on *Billboard's* Mainstream Rock Tracks chart, #9 on the Modern Rock Tracks chart, #78 on the Pop 100, and #84 on the Hot 100.

Another song that got some notice was the memorably titled "You Know What They

Do To Guys Like Us In Prison." This track featured backup vocals from Bert McCracken of The Used. The two bands, having toured together, became friends and this hastened Burt's appearance on My Chem's major-label debut.

Now radio airplay and video rotation was coming fast and furious and the band was no longer just the favorite of New Jersey residents but of people all over the world. Reviews of the album varied from stellar to good. Influential *Rolling Stone* magazine bestowed a three-star review to *Three Cheers*. Kirk Miller reviewed the album for the magazine saying, "Twenty-plus years after The Misfits terrorized New Jersey, their Garden State descendants My Chemical Romance embrace the goth-punk revival in style. *Sweet Revenge* has the same shout-along choruses, speedy drums, and horror themes that fueled Glenn Danzig's old outfit, but it also adds cool metal licks and a sneaky sense of humor (see the thrash-cabaret hybrid "You Know What They Do to Guys Like Us in Prison"). And thanks to frontman Gerard Way's endearing warble, standout tracks such as "Helena" and "I'm Not Okay (I Promise)" come off as more emotion-driven than shock rock. In any case, *Revenge* is a hell of a good time."

The record eventually went Platinum and by April 2006, it had sold over two million copies. In fact, the album sold more records in one week than *Bullets* sold in two whole years! Not bad for a band from an underprivileged town in New Jersey! When asked why *Three Cheers* gained more notoriety than their first record, Gerard suggested to *MetalUnderground.com*, "We had a lot more time to do it. We had a lot more time to write it and we got to develop as a band, really find out who we were before we made another record. On this first record we had only been a band for three months."

It appeared as if nothing could stand in My Chem's way as they topped the charts and became the newest video stars on the block. Sadly, difficult times were ahead.

Chapter 6

DRUGS aNd DRuMMErs

By the summer of July 2004, demand for My Chem in concert was growing. To that end, the band joined the Vans Warped tour. This initially led to some apprehension on Gerard's part as he told Gene Stout of the *Seattle Post-Intelligencer*, "We're not a festival band. Festivals are something completely alien to us. They always have been. So getting on stage the first time at Warped was really terrifying for us. It was like insane. Because we'd never done this. But we probably had one of the best sets of our career that day because we were so nervous. There was such energy."

The concept behind the popular Vans Warped tour was simple: Provide a place where kids could come together and in one afternoon see all their favorite bands and enjoy some extreme sports...all for one low ticket price. Sponsors, such as skateboarding shoe manufacturer Vans, kicked in a lot of money that helped keep the prices so low. Fans loved the format with multiple stages providing a wide variety of music at all times. Gerard maintains that, "Warped is really about kids discovering punk rock." This was indeed the perfect venue to get their music out to the masses.

Indeed, it turned out to be a pivotal tour for My Chem. Again, the pressure mounted. Strangely enough though, the first day of the tour was rained out. "It was like a snow day," Gerard told the *Seattle Post-Intelligencer*. "Then the rain let up, so everyone was hanging out in the parking lot drinking. I think it was a great way to start the tour because everyone got to meet each other and old friends met up again. I got to see guys I hadn't seen in a year because we tour so much. It was like a family reunion."

While the band was publicly enjoying their ride as one of the hottest goth-punk bands on the circuit, behind the scenes they were falling apart. Gerard was slipping deeper and deeper into depression and his drug and alcohol habit was affecting the band.

Thankfully for the band and fans, Gerard recognized his problems and asked for help. "I came to them [the band] and said, 'Look, I have a problem, and I think it's been affecting the band,'" Gerard told MTV. "It was becoming a normal thing for me to drink before the show. And it was something I was very defensive about. But they were really supportive."

Thursday's Geoff Rickly was watching the band carefully during their rise up the charts and worried for his friends. He told the *Alternative Press*, "I can't believe that they're even still a band. Who can go from zero to 120 like that? I heard stories that Gerard was drinking so much and doing so many drugs that I thought, 'Somebody's gonna die; the band's gonna fall apart, and it's gonna be awful.'" He went on to explain how he struggled to figure out what he could do to help. "It's weird to say, because they're a band and they can do what they want but those are our friends. You don't want to see them get sucked into something you've had your band sucked into."

"Any time you mix drinking with narcotics, something bad can happen. And depression—mixing the three of them is really bad." -Frank

Rickly was right to be worried. Around this time, Gerard was going through $150 worth of pills, mostly Xanax, every month and drinking a bottle of vodka every day or so...definitely not a healthy lifestyle, especially for someone who pretty much lived out of a suitcase on the road.

Gerard told the *Alternative Press* how he was able to keep up the pace: "I worked out a system where if we played at noon, I was basically just hung over, still drunk probably from the night before. If we were playing at 1 or 2, I was already drunk. If [I wasn't] fully drunk, then I was trying to get drunk at any signings we had to do. After that, I would continue to get drunk well until the [day's tour stop] was done, until bus call. Bus call would come, or sometimes before it, and I would pop a bunch of Xanax and basically be cracked out. It was the only thing that would put me to sleep and shut my brain off."

The turning point came after one night in the Midwest during My Chem's tour that was co-headlined with Senses Fail. "I had gone to see The Killers and got really drunk. I found a way to get cocaine, and I bought a whole f***ing eight ball and pretty much did the whole f***ing thing," Gerard recalled to *Alternative Press*. "I did so much cocaine that I was in the middle of the street throwing up everywhere. My head was pounding; it felt twice its size. All the veins in my head felt like they were going to explode. The next day, I woke up, and I was more suicidal that morning than I had ever been in my entire life—and it was completely amazing to me. Nobody in my band knew. I had a really good way of hiding stuff."

Brian Schechter, the band's manager, talked Gerard out of his suicidal mood during an intense phone call, but the singer was still unsure about his future. The band was set to go to Japan for a few shows and he was scared: "I was terrified," admitted Gerard to the *Alternative Press*. "All I did was sweat two days before Japan. I sweated buckets, drank, and loaded up on my pills for the trip." Indeed, Gerard took so much Xanax before the flight he has no idea how he even made it to Japan. He also drank a lot in country and played the two shows completely wasted.

"My intention was to make it a memorable experience for everyone and I did," he says. "But it's kind of like making a deal with the devil. I sure made it a memorable experience for everyone—but in the worse possible way."

Meanwhile, the band was becoming hip to just how much of a problem Gerard's wild lifestyle was becoming. "It's weird, because usually, when we're playing, me and

Gerard can look at each other and no matter what's going on, I can pull back to it and go for it," said guitarist Frank Iero. "When I looked for him [in Osaka] and he was underneath the stage being drunk, I just wanted to [put my guitar down] and go."

Could the band really not have seen the writing on the wall before this? Mikey admits that he knew about his brother's problems. "I think I was accepting because I was equally bad as he was at one point," he told the *Alternative Press*. "I was even worse than him at some points early on in the band's career. I thought it'd be really hypocritical to say, 'Put that vodka down!'" But the entire band knew the drug use was growing and would come to a head eventually. As Frank suggested to the *Alternative Press*, "Any time you mix drinking with narcotics, something bad can happen. And depression—mixing the three of them is really bad. Every time you do it, it changes your whole body chemistry. When we were touring, no one really thought about it, because we were all doing it together."

The Japanese shows turned out to be a low point for the entire band. "I walked offstage and I threw up for 45 minutes straight in this garbage can, like I had never thrown up before," said Gerard. "I puked everything out. The whole band was there, and I was sitting on the couch in the corner. Ray turns to Brian [Schechter, the band's manager] and says, 'You need to get him to the doctor. Listen to him. He's not doing well. There's something wrong with him. He's really sick.' Sitting there, I still have vomit all over myself, and I just thought this has to be the end. I was still really suicidal and depressed, but I was just like, I have to stop drinking. I don't know how,

but this has to be the end. I didn't know what was going to happen when I got back to the U.S. I got off the plane and was really upset."

Adding to Gerard's depression was the fact that the band was planning on ditching drummer Matt Pelissier. While the five band members had a brotherly relationship with each other, the guys were becoming frustrated with Matt's playing. They maintain that he was messing up onstage and they no longer felt he was the right drummer for My Chem. His last performances with the group would be in Japan and then he'd be fired. "I knew what was going to happen to Otter [Matt Pelissier], and I think that's another reason why I was really upset," noted Gerard. "I said goodbye to him [in Japan] and knew that I probably was not going to see him again. At the same time, I didn't know if I was going to be alive the next day. I said goodbye to everybody and I had tears in my eyes because I wasn't really sure if I was going to see anyone in my band again."

The parting between Matt and the band did not go well and was not amicable. This was mainly due to the way My Chem imparted the news to Matt. It came as a complete shock to him. Guitarist Ray Toro spoke with the *Alternative Press* about it saying, "It was like the moment that you break up with someone you've been dating for three or four years that you used to love in the beginning of the relationship and things went sour, but for some reason you're still together." Ray and band manager Brian Schechter went to Matt's house in Jersey to fire him in person.

"I was flat-out told the only reason I'm being kicked out of the band is because, 'We don't feel comfortable with you onstage anymore because one, you don't play to the click track, and two, these couple times you messed up, we just don't feel comfortable.' Even though Gerard was drunk every night and messed up every night...," Matt drifted off, part of him sad and part irritated. The entire situation left him cold. "The last time I saw or heard from Gerard, it was when I gave him a hug at the airport [after two shows in Japan]," he explained to the *Alternative Press*.

"I had Ray come up to me once or twice and ask me to play to a click track live, and I said no. Pretty much no drummer does, because it takes away the whole live feeling. And that was it. I got back from Japan, and only Ray came to my house with Schechter. It's like your whole world comes crashing down, after I gave everything I ever did, everything I ever owned to make sure that band would survive," asserted Matt, "and that's the thanks I get."

Even though some time has passed, the hard feelings have not. In fact, Frank is the only band member that has talked with Pelissier since Japan. "I called him right after it happened," Frank said, "and was like, 'Yo, I wanted to be there, but I understand why Ray wanted to talk to you alone. I hope that we can be mature about this after everything blows over. I hope you keep playing music, but I'm sorry that it had to go down this way. Call me if you ever want to." Matt has no plans to rekindle his friendship with any of the guys in My Chem.

At the time, the band was a bit squeamish about announcing a change in lineup. "People probably thought it was weird that we didn't make any kind of statement beforehand or really talk about what happened," Ray reflected. "It must've been weird for people to notice, 'Wow! One of the members who started the band and has been in the band for three years is now gone, and they haven't said anything.' The main reason why we decided to do that is because we didn't want to get into a pissing match, and we didn't want to have this sort of he-said, she-said bullshit. There are obviously things that went along with that decision, like a lack of getting along with him and a lack of being able to play songs the same way every night. But the main reason was that we weren't having fun being in the band. He had to have known in his heart—whether he'll admit or not—that he wasn't performing up to the way we needed to perform. You had to have been f***ing blind to not see the relationship problems between each of us and him—that we just didn't get along. When I started getting into the reasons of why we made the decision, he just walked away. That was the last time I spoke to him."

The shakeup affected everyone in the band but My Chem has moved past it. As for Gerard, those days were actually quite cathartic. After the Japan fiasco, he got a therapist and hasn't drank or taken a pill since. For his sake, and for the sake of My Chem fans the world over, let's hope it stays that way!

Chapter 7
AND theN THeRE WaS Bob

With Japan behind them and Matt out of the picture, My Chemical Romance now had to find a new drummer. They found the perfect replacement in Brian Bryar, who was previously a soundman for The Used. He'd met the band before and had admired their work. "It was at Irving Plaza, maybe a year and a half ago," admitted Bryar, "and My Chemical Romance [were playing with] Finch and The Used. My Chem finished playing, and I walked into the back and said something to [their manager] like, 'I wish I could do that.'" It was lucky for MCR that Bryar was so enthusiastic and available to jump into Matt's shows at a moment's notice.

Bob is the only member of My Chem who did not grow up in Jersey. He was born on New Year's Eve 1979 in Chicago as Robert Nathaniel Bryar. He learned to play drums when he was just a kid and even played in the jazz band at Eisenhower Junior High in Darien, Illinois. He did go to college for a while in Gainesville, Florida and even worked at Walt Disney World for a bit!

Frank Iero immediately felt Bob was a match made in heaven for My Chem, "Bob and Toro are the two hardest working people I've ever met, and if there is a God, I thank him every day for bringing us Bob."

Through the summer and fall of 2004, the band continued to tour and played one particularly infamous show in the parking lot of Best Buy in Orange, California. The free show sponsored by radio station KROQ-FM was staged as a thank-you to local

"Bob and Toro are the two hardest working people i've ever met, and if there is a God, i thank him every day for bringing us Bob." -Frank

fans. (The Donnas opened for My Chem). But clashes between the band and police made the event uncomfortable for the band. Gerard told MTV, "The Orange Police said that we were trying to incite a riot and that we used excessive foul language, and they threatened to arrest us for trespassing. They were giving us a hard time all day. And after we finished playing, the police said that we would never be allowed to play in the city of Orange again."

Police were frustrated with My Chem for several reasons: 1. Their use of vulgar language in a public venue. 2. Their promise to fans to meet and greet everyone after the show. Unfortunately, too many fans showed up and the band wasn't able to keep its promise. Local police were forcing the band off the property by 5 p.m. and so thousands of fans were turned away before having a chance to meet the guys. Gerard said, "It took 15 security guards to get all the fans to leave the parking lot. It was probably the biggest bum-out of our career."

In September, the band appeared on MTV2's *Advance Warning* with Rachael Yamagata, Keane, Jim Jones, Matchbook Romance, Slim Thug, Rupee, and Hope Of The States. They also played the Nintendo Fusion tour, an event where fans can listen to their favorite bands and preview new video games and equipment. The guys sounded fantastic on this tour, in part because of Gerard's new drug-free lifestyle and partly because of their new drummer Bob. Gerard warned MTV that, "A lot has changed since our last tour. I got clean and sober. And it made the shows change dramatically, because my singing got a lot better. I used to drink pretty heavily in general and before shows, and that stopped. Alcohol is a depressant, so it was putting me in a really bad spot, mentally. I couldn't really tour anymore if I was going to be depressed and drunk."

With terrific concert reviews, the band caught some momentum and reveled in additional record sales while constantly touring. On September 21, Vagrant Records released the two-disc *In Honor: A Compilation To Beat Cancer*. My Chem joined 41 other bands that each contributed a song to this worthy cause. It's a great CD to add to your collection as it highlights My Chem, The Descendants, Face To Face, Jawbreaker, Thursday, Saves The Day, The Bouncing Souls, None More Black, Thrice, Taking Back Sunday, and a slew of other hot punk rockers.

That November, the band once again played at Irving Plaza in New York City's Union Square area. My Chemical Romance closed out 2004 with an appearance on the second night of KROQ's Almost Acoustic Christmas concert. They played alongside Green Day, Incubus, Sum 41, Hoobastank, Velvet Revolver, Good Charlotte, Social Distortion, The Used, Papa Roach, and Chevelle. Proceeds from the event went to Para Los Ninos, an organization that helps children living in poverty in the Los Angeles area.

Chapter 8

tHE RoaD to SuccESs

By early 2005, the genie was definitely out of the bottle and fans the world over were clamoring for more music from My Chemical Romance. The band set up an aggressive tour schedule that lasted all year. They had definitely come a long way from the early days when they toured in an old 15-passenger van! Now the band was playing to thousands of people every night and having a blast doing it.

They started the year with a benefit concert for the Indonesian tsunami victims. [A catastrophic tsunami hit Sumatra, Indonesia and nearby areas on December 26, 2004. More than 275,000 people were killed.] The show, part of the Concerts for Tsunami Relief, was held at the Starland Ballroom in Sayreville, N.J. and featured headliner Taking Back Sunday with MCR, Coheed and Cambria, Senses Fail, The Banner, and Like Yesterday. Tickets sold out in a mere five minutes and were later to be found on eBay for as much as $200 a piece. The concert was co-sponsored by Linkin Park's Music for Relief charity organization and New York radio station K-ROCK. When all was said and done, the concert raised $75,000 in ticket sales and K-Rock kicked in an additional $20k. MTV covered the event and noted that Gerard was especially theatrical that evening, making lots of "gun-to-head" gestures. MCR, not surprisingly, closed their performance with "I'm Not Okay (I Promise)."

Having done their civic duty, the band was now ready to hit the road for a 38-city extravaganza in the form of the Taste of Chaos tour. The brainchild of Kevin Lyman, who also runs the Vans Warped tour, Taste of Chaos was devised as an emo festival that would visit arenas during the cold-weather months. The main stage lineup included The Used, MCR, Killswitch Engage, Senses Fail, Static Lullaby, and Underoath for the East Coast dates and Saosin for the West. Secondary acts were Second State, Bleed The Dream, and Opiate For The Masses. The caravan hit the road in February, opening the tour in Orlando on the 18. Taste of Chaos rolled across the U.S. and eventually slammed to a halt on April 2 in Phoenix, Arizona.

During the tour, My Chem was extremely friendly with members of The Used. That led to the bands pooling their resources to record an updated rendition of Queen and David Bowie's 1981 hit "Under Pressure." In March, the two bands appeared on MTV's

"This is a dream come true. i have wanted to tour with Green Day since i was 15."
-Frank

$2 Bill show to sing the song. Fans loved it and encouraged the bands to release the song, which they did the following month in April 2005. Gerard told MTV, "It [the recorded song] sounds awesome, and now it's just a matter of getting it ready. We've played it live with [The Used on Taste of Chaos], just to make people aware of it, and when it becomes available, all the proceeds are going to charity." It was released as a digital download to benefit the tsunami victims. Gerard also talked with *Billboard* about the release: "My Chemical Romance couldn't wait to release the studio version because we feel it's important to contribute to a worthwhile cause, and some people may overlook tsunami relief now that three months have passed."

More good news arrived for the band in April when *Three Cheers For Sweet Revenge* peaked the *Billboard* 200 album chart at #45. That was all well and good but what really had the band stoked was the fact that Green Day, a band they idolized, had invited them on tour! Gerarld even told MTV that this is "...the biggest thing to ever happen to this band." My Chem didn't hesitate to sign on to open for Green Day during their North American tour that started on April 15 in Coral Gables, Florida.

It wasn't just Gerard that was psyched about working with Green Day. Guitarist Frank Iero told Darin Longman of *University Wire* that, "The tour is unreal. I have said this before, but it is completely true: This is a dream come true. I have wanted to tour with Green Day since I was 15. For them to choose us is mind-blowing. [Green Day] is

one of those bands that trail-blazed so much. If it weren't for Green Day, bands like us or any band wouldn't be able to reach the heights that we have reached here. They opened up so many doors for real bands to come in and reach their goals. It is flattering that they would take us out on tour. It is very validating."

Every single member of My Chem had been influenced by Green Day on some level, so this tour was special. "Oh man. Billie Joe from Green Day influenced everything about how I play guitar. He just made it look so easy. He was the first person I aped," Gerard told MTV. "And if it wasn't for Green Day I wouldn't have picked up a guitar. The band couldn't believe it when we heard the news [opening for Green Day]. I got the call and I was in the street in New York City and it was pouring rain, but I was just yelling and people were staring at me. And that was everybody's response. I think Bob [Bryar] fell down a flight of stairs when he heard the news."

With all the excitement, you'd think the band would just focus on the tour. But, they had more on their minds and jury-rigged a studio in their tour bus so they could begin writing and recording demos for their next record. Guitarist Ray Toro told MTV,

"We've written five to six skeletons of songs. We're trying to get to a level where we can get the songs into the studio and sort of flesh them out in there. We're always writing because we're dying to finish a new record." With laser focus, the guys set their ideas down as they rolled across America.

Gerard was particularly happy with the new songs, telling MTV, "I feel so extremely confident in the direction we're moving in, because we made a great leap from *I Brought You My Bullets, You Brought Me Your Love* to *Revenge*, and that leap can be even greater now. I feel it moving in a very mature, big rock type of thing. It feels more direct and honest, and I'm very excited by it. I can't wait." Fans couldn't either. Live music was one thing but their loyal legions were also dying for new recorded music to load up in their MP3 players.

"We've got about eight songs written for the next record, and we love all of them," announced Gerard to MTV. "It's a reflection of the band maturing. The band knows what it does well, and it still does that, but we're taking a few risks. Some slower tempos, some heavier stuff. There's more of the arena-rock element that was hinted on with the last record."

In *Rolling Stone* Gerard said, "We don't want to milk this record [*Three Cheers*]. This record was a success, but we want to leave it at that and go on and do other records for our fans, who have had this record for a year now. It's moving in more of an arena-rock direction. *Revenge* was a punk band, but a punk band that looked up to Smashing Pumpkins. It's now moving into a fuller arena-rock sound. They're all really beautiful songs. It's real honest stuff. There's less fiction and more about our lives. I think it's important that this band be able to relate to human beings, because our lives have just gotten crazy. There's a lot of stuff that's happening in our lives now—it's not about eating, shitting, and breathing your band. You're being a human being again."

At the end of May, My Chem headlined the first Bamboozle Festival in Asbury Park, New Jersey with Brand New, Alkaline Trio, Thrice, The Starting Line, Fall Out Boy, The Bouncing Souls, Straylight Run, and Flogging Molly. Fifty other acts were also on the bill for this three-day event that took place at several venues including the Stone Pony, Convention Hall, and Bradley Park. It was competing for fans with the Coachella Festival that was staged the same weekend in Indio, California. The big difference was the ticket price. Bamboozle set fans back just $79 for three days while Coachella soaked music lovers for $150 for a two-day pass. MCR fans were overjoyed that their band was playing Bamboozle!

Further catering to their fans late that month, My Chem released a video game version of "Helena" on their Web site, *www.mychemicalromance.com*. The game was a nod to the old days and was reminiscent of Dig Dug or Joust. The audio includes a three-note rendition of "Helena" and players control a corpse as she makes her way through a maze. All in all, a unique way to market an emo tune!

Continuing on the "Helena" theme, the band played two shows in one day at the London Astoria. While fans queued up outside the club, an antique hearse drove by, followed by a funeral procession of fans in Victorian dress. One fan even acted the part of Helena and laid in the coffin surrounded by flowers. That night, a floral display spelling out "Helena" added some sparkle to the stage set.

After the memorable London shows, the band then returned to the states for KROQ's thirteenth annual Weenie Roast in Los Angeles where they played to a packed crowd on May 21. Other bands on the bill included Alkaline Trio, Audioslave, Foo Fighters, Jimmy Eat World, The Killers, Motley Crue, Queens Of The Stone Age, and others.

The one downside of the month of May came when MCR's new video for "The Ghost Of You" was leaked to the public before it was fully edited. "The video is set in World

War II, and it's really about...loss and the fear of losing people, so we wanted the video to reflect war and loss and love and everything," Gerard told MTV. "I had a conversation with Marc [Webb, director] during the 'Helena' video about the treatment idea I had. And then I wrote it out-one and a half pages-and sent it to him, and he fleshed it out."

"Gerard had this idea for awhile," director Marc Webb later told MTV. "The main thrust is that it takes place in World War II, and there's a USO dance and these combat sequences too. The USO dance happens during the verses of the song, and the combat sequences happen during the chorus, because there's a big dichotomy between those two parts of the song. When we talked about making 'Ghost Of You,' we spoke of it being very cinematic. Our goal for this was to make it feel like you're watching a film and creating a world. The guitar playing and singing is an organic part of them playing in the USO scene. And there are a handful of battlefield scenes. And there's a huge, epic quality to the piece. It's something you just don't get to see on MTV. It's a period piece, and we tried really hard to be genuine and authentic. So the band [is] in the appropriate uniforms, and we cut their hair. We did everything all the way. From the beginning, I was telling Gerard, 'We gotta cut your hair,' and literally hours after they performed at the [KROQ] Weenie Roast, he cut it short. It's not an Army-style crew cut, but it's close. You'll see."

Marc went on to say that, "This is the biggest video I've ever done. It's the biggest video they've ever done. And it's probably the biggest rock video to have come along in years. It's a really big deal to them. They're a theatrical band, and the ideal of showmanship is very important to them. And if this video is anything, it's theatrical. It's got war and loss and love and camaraderie and everything."

The video made its premier during the pre-show of the 2005 MTV Video Music Awards. It was clear that Gerard and all of My Chem were referencing movies such as *Saving Private Ryan* and *Memphis Belle*. Many scenes in the video showed the guys wearing army fatigues.

The video was going to be epic and the band was so proud of their work. That's why it was a drag when the video was leaked to the public before they felt it was ready to be seen. Gerard kept a positive attitude about the debacle telling MTV, "It's not a bad problem to have people wanting to see our video so badly that they're trying to find it on the Internet or leak it. Sure you're bummed artistically, because it's not finished, but it's a pretty awesome problem. There's so much buzz about it that people can't wait."

Frank explained it to MTV like this: "It's like paining a picture, and you're not done with it yet, but someone shows it in an art exhibit. It's the art that you make, and if you don't feel that it's done, for people to go and put it on the Internet and have people download it is a bit of a bummer. It was pretty much finished, but there were still little finishing touches that if you saw it now, you wouldn't even notice they were there, but I noticed them."

When all was said and done, fans loved both the unofficial and official versions of the video for "The Ghost Of You." The band needn't have worried!
On June 17, they blasted off on the eleventh annual Vans Warped tour. This summer, they toured alongside Transplants, Thrice, and Fall Out Boys. The tour opened at the German Amphitheatre in Columbus, Ohio and brought the boys back to Englishtown Raceway in Asbury Park, New Jersey on August 14 for the final show. Even though they weren't the headliners, My Chem and Fall Out Boys turned out to be the stars of this tour.

Matt Skiba of Alkaline Trio told the *Alternative Press* what it was like seeing My Chem on stage during the tour: "I wandered out into the crowd, [MCR] started playing, and I got kind of the same feeling that I got going to Naked Raygun shows. They were so good and sounded so great, and the energy exchange with the crowd was something that I hadn't seen in a long time. I had no choice. I had to start dancing. My drink was full when I walked in there, and five second later, it was all over a bunch of kids' heads."

During the band's downtime, they played Dungeons & Dragons with the guys in Thrice. "Its about the nerdiest thing you can do," admitted Dustin Kensrue, Thrice's lead singer, to *Rolling Stone*, "so we're gonna dive in." Despite the laid-back tone and

socializing during off-hours, MCR never forgot to give it their all on stage. "For a lot of kids, it's the one thing [Vans Warped tour] they look forward to all year," Gerard told *Rolling Stone*. "They save up for it. They get to see all the bands they like on one shot." My Chem was especially thankful to fans during this tour since the band had made such strides since the summer before. "Last year we played the second stage—it's really a big change," noted Gerard. "It's cool that a band that's been around as long as The Offspring is willing to share the stage."

You'd think with their intense schedule of touring and writing songs, band members would be stretched to the limit. Not so. In fact, in July of 2005, Frank even found time to launch Skelton Crew, his own record label, book publisher, and clothing company. This is the "manifesto" from the company's Web site, *www.skeletoncrewonline.com*: "In a world of mainstream, sub and counter cultures, attitudes change quickly. The Skeleton Crew ideology is to design and create products that sculpt a new way of living. We are pioneering an infectious sustainable culture involving music, clothing, art and literature. In each endeavor, we promise to infuse our value of hard work and dedication to a cause much larger than personal gain. Some of our proceeds will be donated to an organization of the contributing artist's choice—because we believe that everyone has a responsibility to make a change in their lifetime. As individuals who have been influenced by the movements of creative minds, our goal is to

contribute to the spawning of unique independent thinkers who live everyday like it's their last."

Frank was thrilled with his new venture and was even more pumped when he heard that *Three Cheers For Sweet Revenge* had sold more than 826,000 copies by the end of July. The band was definitely riding high!

On August 24, My Chem fans got a new song from their favorite band in the form of "Astro Zombies." It was just one of the songs included on *Tony Hawk's American Wasteland Soundtrack* CD. The video game soundtrack CD featured original recordings from My Chem, Fall Out Boy, Taking Back Sunday, Senses Fail, Thrice, Alkaline Trio, and others. Activision and Vagrant Records released the record. It's a choice CD for your collection.

The band found itself in the U.K. again in late August, playing the Carling Weekend: Leeds Festival on the 25th. This was a three-day event headlined by Pearl Jam. Before taking the stage, the band found out that they'd won two Kerrang! Awards: Best Video

("Helena") and Best Album (*Three Cheers For Sweet Revenge*) from *Kerrang!* magazine. My Chem knocked out a 45-minute set and played a few new songs from *The Black Parade* including "Dead," "House Of Wolves," and "Cancer."

Speaking of awards, on August 28 the band hustled back to the U.S. for MTV's Video Music Awards at Miami's American Airlines Arena. They arrived in style in a Brinks Security truck! Diddy hosted the event and performers included Kanye West, Kelly Clarkson, and Green Day. My Chem performed "Helena" and were nominated for several awards but unfortunately didn't win anything. According to *Rolling Stone*, when Fall Out Boy's bassist/lyricist Pete Wentz accepted the MTV2 Award for "Sugar, We're Going Down," he said MCR should have won for "Helena." That's what fans thought too.

With all the accolades and press coverage, My Chem was getting antsy to embark on their very first headline tour. And, that dream came true in mid-September 2005. The band drafted OGs, Alkaline Trio, and Reggie And The Full Effect as opening bands. The 30-city tour started at the PromoWest Pavilion in Columbus, Ohio and ended at the McKay Events Center in Baltimore, Maryland. Jersey fans were also treated to two shows in their state: an October 13 gig at Continental Arena in East Rutherford and an October 14 show at the Tweeter Center in Camden, near Philadelphia.

The band was so excited about their first headline tour that they began telling the media all about their visions for an ultra-theatrical stage set and show. In an interview with *Billboard* magazine, Ray Toro said, "It's just great to have a visual connection to music and I think that's definitely something that's been missing from rock 'n' roll. A lot of bands these days don't work on creating an image for their band and their videos. We're looking to do that for our live shows too. We're going to kind of have a visual element to go along with the music. We're really interested in actually putting on a show. Bands get on stage, play their songs, and have some lights, and that's cool, but we really want to try to take it to the next level."

Unfortunately, their ideas were more lavish than reality would allow and they needed to tamp back their statements. "We talked about bringing out dancers for our headlining tour in the fall," Gerard explained to MTV, "but it's a big undertaking; you have to have a bus full of dancers. We've always wanted to do a big theatrical tour. But you have to do it in steps. You just can't spring it on people all at once. So we've been working on video content and lighting for the fall tour—just some stuff we've never had. And hopefully with our next U.S. tour—which might be for our next album—we'll have some real theatrical stuff."

He went on to say, "We're a very passionate band—our show is very kinetic, so we don't want people to be watching a whole lot of video. We want you to be watching us. That being said, we've taken our ambitious ideas and broken them down into something I don't think anyone has seen before. We're going to be using a lot of video content and shapes and visual elements. We want to give people a full night with us, and we want to give some fans who've known us for a long time the chance to hear some of those older songs that they never get to hear, ever. We've always wanted to give something back to our fans and to play the kind of shows we know they want to see. And we really think this tour is exactly that."

September saw a change of pace for Gerard as he helped out some friends and wrote a video treatment for Thrice's "Image Of The Invisible." Thrice frontman Dustin Kensrue and Gerard are longtime friends and while on the road during the Warped tour, they brainstormed ideas for the video. The idea was Kensrue's, but Gerard developed it and wrote the actual treatment.

Teppei Teranishi, guitarist for Thrice told MTV, "Dustin came up with the real general treatment, and this summer he and Gerard kind of went back and forth and came up with a more concise treatment." Kensrue concurred: "I sat down with Gerard and we brainstormed, and the children being stolen started coming in as a motif, so we started stealing some of the aesthetics from *The City Of Lost Children*—sort of that surreal atmosphere. The Watchers and the resistance, that was always in my head, but it got more refined. Gerard was helping me get the details down so it would feel right. It came together after that. We just started honing it until it felt like it was all working."

Jay Martin directed the futuristic video that tells the story of an evil organization called The Watchers who snatch children. It's definitely reminiscent of 1995's *The City Of Lost Children*. Thrice play the part of freedom fighters trying to get the children back.

"We were all really excited to have him [Gerard] be a part of it and contribute to the creative vision of the video," Thrice drummer Riley Breckenridge told MTV. "You look at all the videos My Chem's done, and they're all really cool and cinematic. Gerard has a really interesting way of seeing things. He used to be an artist and do comic books and stuff, and now he's a big movie buff. He had a big role in getting Dustin's vision focused and enhancing the visual elements."

Also in September, Gerard collaborated with Thursday's Geoff Rickly on his follow up to the 2003 album, *War All The Time*. The record, *A City By The Light Divided*, was produced by Dave Fridmann at Tarbox Road Studios in Fredonia, New York. Geoff had produced My Chem's *I Brought You My Bullets, You Brought Me Your Love*. Now it was time for Gerard to repay the favor. "I sort of helped My Chem start their whole thing up, and now that they're huge, I don't want to exploit that," Geoff cautiously told MTV. "He's a friend of mine, and if it ended up seeming exploitative—like he did something with us and the label wanted to use it as a single—it would be too weird." *A City By The Light Divided* was released in 2006 to rave reviews.

At the end of October, My Chem was to play the Voodoo Music Experience in New Orleans with Queens Of The Stone Age, The Flaming Lips, Billy Idol, The New York Dolls, Secret Machines, DJ Tiesto, The Bravery, Ryan Adams, and Mickey Hart's Voodoo Drum Circle. However, Hurricane Katrina had other plans for them. The band cancelled their appearance at the festival. Part of the show went on as scheduled in New Orleans, on a much smaller scale, and part of the event was moved to Memphis.

The cancellation was just as well because the band was scrambling to get ready for their British / European tour which blasted off on November 1. Gerard told the *Alternative Press* that My Chem always enjoys playing the U.K. "British people really get black humor, and that's one of the strongest elements [of our band]," he said. "I think they heard emo and wanted something different. We are kind of the 'What else you got?' of emo."

In an interview with Elisa Bray of *The Independent*, Gerard reinforces his ideas about the U.K.: "Britain was the first country that accepted us. It's because our influences all lie in British roots: The Smiths, Iron Maiden, The Cure, Pulp, Oasis, Blur. The only

American bands we are influenced by have been punk bands, all other aspects come from British music."

While on the road, the band found out they won Woodie of the Year (aka Artist of the Year) at the second annual mtvU Awards. Voted by college students across the U.S. via *mtvu.com*, My Chem was up against Arcade Fire. The awards ceremony took place at Roseland Ballroom in Manhattan with Lou Reed opening the show and actor Philip Seymour Hoffman MCing.

Magazines and newspapers reported on the band's big win at the mtvU Awards, but they also published stories about a growing riff between Gerard and The Used's lead singer Bert McCracken. The two had been close friends but something had changed. In an interview with MTV, McCracken gravely said, "I'd prefer not to say anything about My Chemical Romance, except that we did have a falling out. We don't speak at all anymore. It's got nothing to do with their success. I'm completely comfortable with where our band is at. We used to be very close, but no more. We had a falling out. The rest of my band, they're still mates with all the guys in that band. But I'd prefer to say nothing more about My Chemical Romance."

It was a sad way to close out the year and fans never really did get the full story on what went down that contributed to the crumbling of the friendship. Gerard probably didn't have much time to dwell on the matter though. 2006 was already promising to be a year to remember for his band.

Chapter 9

liFe On tHe MuRdER scEne

2006 saw the band in New York City doing pre-production for their forthcoming studio album. Fans couldn't be happier knowing they'd soon get new My Chem songs! The band also hooked them up with a remix of "To The End." The song—remixed by Black Light Burns (Wes Borland of Limp Bizkit, Danny Lohner of Nine Inch Nails, Josh Freeze of A Perfect Circle, and Josh Eustis of Telefon Tel Aviv)—was included on the soundtrack CD for the movie *Underworld*.

In February My Chem took some time out of their schedule to talk with reporters about new action figures that were released in their image by SEG Toys of Schaumburg, Illinois. These 5-inch-tall bendable, pose-able action figures of MCR band members are each packaged in a coffin and come with a red handgun. The band joined the ranks of Metallica, Green Day, and Good Charlotte—all of whom had been previously immortalized in doll figure.

Gerard told MTV, "We hate when people call us 'dolls.' We're definitely action figures. We're a little bigger than Star Wars [figures] and fully articulated, and our faces are digitally scanned. They're very realistic. We're wearing suits and we've got elbow joints. They're really pose-able and rad. You can make them do things like shake violently or save a cat from a tree." He went on to say, "...what we would really love is for people to see that even regular people can end up as toys. You just have to chase it." What a modest statement!

In February, Gerard designed a limited edition Gothic-style blazer. The proceeds of the sale benefited Boarding for Breast Cancer, a nonprofit organization that tries to increase awareness about breast cancer. Only 600 jackets—called "Prom Knight"— were made and were sold at *SmartPunk.com*. Gerard told MTV that his design was, "...something casual yet formal...kind of sleek. Something a gentleman would wear to a duel." Indeed!

That same month saw My Chem sweep the 2005 *Spin* Readers Poll with wins in the following categories: Band of the Year, Song of the Year ("Helena"), Cover of the Year (they won both best and worse), Sex God [for Gerard], and Best Live Act.

Gerard told *Spin* that he felt a bit silly about being named "Sex God." "I can't honestly say what makes me sexy...I don't feel very sexy...that whole part of it is weird...seeing yourself, a recovering drug addict and alcoholic, on the cover of *Teen Beat*...it doesn't make any sense," he said. "I am who I am...there's no façade...no put on...and being voted sexiest doesn't concern me...maybe that's the sexy part."

He went on to talk about how proud the band was to win Best Live Act. "That is probably the greatest honor," he

> **"i can't honestly say what makes me sexy...i don't feel very sexy."**
> **-Gerard**

admitted. "To win Best Live Act is exhilarating. We got good because the kids got good, and we work our asses off. There's nothing rehearsed, synchronized, or planned—it is a live show in the very sense of the world. When we play live, it's like saying, 'We mean this more than anything. This may be the last time we ever take a stage, so don't f*** with us.'"

More awards poured in on February 25 at MTV's fourth annual TRL Awards. Hosted by *TLR's* Damien Fahey, Vanessa Minnillo, and Susie Castillo, Gerard was nominated for Man of the Year against Kanye West, Eminem, and 50 Cent. The band was also nominated as Best New Artist against Ciara, Fall Out Boy, and Brown.
Showing their philanthropic side once again, the band played a March 17 benefit concert—their first gig of 2006—during South by Southwest in Austin to benefit Shirts for a Cure (*www.shirtsforacure.com*). According to the nonprofit's Web site, "The Syrentha J. Savio Endowment (SSE) was established by punk-rock photographer Mark Beemer in 2002. SSE provides financial assistance to underprivileged women who cannot afford expensive breast cancer medicine and therapy. Because SSE is active within the punk rock community, the Shirts For A Cure project was launched to give

voice to the social concerns of punk bands and their many fans. When a band donates a shirt design, the design becomes an SSE exclusive. We sell the shirt and use the proceeds to help women fighting breast cancer."

As April approached, fans were eagerly awaiting the next My Chem release, a one CD / two-DVD set titled *Life On The Murder Scene*. Released by Reprise / Warner on March 21, the audio CD included the following live tracks: "Thank You For The Venom" / "Cemetery Drive" / "Give 'Em Hell, Kid" / "Headfirst For Halos" / "Helena" / "You Know What They Do To Guys Like Us In Prison" / "The Ghost Of You" / "I'm Not Okay (I Promise)" / "I Never Told You What I Do For A Living" (demo) / "Bury Me In Black" (demo) / and "Desert Song" (previously unreleased). This set would tie fans over until the new record was ready in October.

Tracks 1 through 3 were from MTV's *$2 Bill* show, track 4 was a live performance from the Starland Ballroom in New Jersey, tracks 5 through 8 were from AOL Sessions recorded on February 17, 2004, tracks 9 and 10 were recorded at the Shed in NYC in

December 2003 by Daniel Wise, and track 11 was produced by Howard Benson. At My Chem's Web site, the band posted the following note to fans about the new video/diary set:

"To all the friends we've made,

Thank you so much for your love and support, your letters and Twizzlers, your homemade awards and creepy stuffed animals. Over the past few years, you have touched our hearts and let us know we are not alone in this world. For awhile now we have wanted to let you all know how much you mean to us...something from our hearts to yours. We decided making each and everyone one of you a plate of brownies was not the answer. So instead we decided to let you in on our story...the truth about everything. Where we came from, what we've been through, and who we truly are, five friends who tried their best to make a difference in this world. Thank you for listening, screaming, dancing, being yourself, and for making us a part of your lives. Know that when you say, 'MCR saved my life,' the feeling is mutual. When we felt too tired to carry on, you gave us purpose to continue. We are forever thankful for all of you. So enjoy this chronicle of the past few years, and lets dry our eyes and move on together. --Xoxo, MCR"

As for the DVDs, the first was a "video diary" with lots of rare footage of all the band members. DVD Two featured four hours of footage from 2002 through 2004, including:

Live Performances
"I'm Not Okay (I Promise)"—Starland Ballroom, N.J.
"Cemetery Drive"—Starland Ballroom, N.J.
"Our Lady Of Sorrows"—Starland Ballroom, N.J.
"Honey, This Mirror Isn't Big Enough For The Two Of Us"—MTV2 *$2 Bill* show
"You Know What They Do To Guys Like Us In Prison"—MTV2 *$2 Bill* show

"Headfirst For Halos"—Starland Ballroom, N.J.
"The Ghost Of You"—MTV2 *$2 Bill* show
"Thank You For The Venom"—Starland Ballroom, N.J.
"Give 'Em Hell, Kid"—MTV2 *$2 Bill* show
"Vampires Will Never Hurt You"—Starland Ballroom, N.J.
"Helena"—Starland Ballroom, N.J.

TV Appearances
"I'm Not Okay (I Promise)"—From MTV *Discover And Download*
"I'm Not Okay (I Promise)"—*Late Night With Conan O'Brien*

Online Performances
"Helena"—*Live At The AOL Sessions*

"I'm Not Okay (I Promise)—*Live At The AOL Sessions*
"The Ghost Of You"—*Live At The AOL Sessions*
"You Know What They Do To Guys Like Us In Prison"—*Live At Launch*
"I'm Not Okay (I Promise)"—*Live At Launch*
"Helena"—*Live At Launch*

Videos
"I'm Not Okay (I Promise)"—Directed by Greg Kaplan
"I'm Not Okay (I Promise)"—Directed by Marc Webb
Making the Video "I'm Not Okay (I Promise)"—Directed by Michael Mihal/Guerilla Hollywood
"The Ghost Of You"—Directed by Marc Webb
Making the Video "The Ghost Of You"—Directed by Michael Mihal/Guerilla Hollywood

In addition to including video clips from 2002 to 2004 during the making of *Three Cheers For Sweet Revenge*, the video diary also shows Gerard battling his cocaine and alcohol addiction. While he is now clean and sober, it took a lot of guts to show this very personal side of his life to fans.

In the liner notes for the album, the band wrote, "You hold in your hands the story of five kids who have had their dreams come true. We would like to dedicate this release to our families and loved ones who've believed in us from the beginning. To all of our friends who work tirelessly to keep MCR dangerous, and to the fans...This is for you. Thank you from the bottom of our black little hearts for staying so pure, so passionate, and so strong. Your belief in us is immeasurable and for that we love you eternally."

Fans reciprocated that love by pushing *Life On The Murder Scene* to enter and peak the *Billboard* 200 album chart at #30. The release also received a three-star review from Rolling Stone. In the March 9 issue, music journalist Jenny Eliscu wrote, "Just because the gothed-out Jersey boys in My Chemical Romance can now fill arenas doesn't mean their hearts aren't still in the mildewed basements where they got their start playing DIY hardcore shows. As this live set shows, My Chem remain a punk band, and their flashes of reckless, claws-bared greatness tend to happen outside the studio, in front of the fans. *Life On The Murder Scene*, which also includes two DVDs collecting video diaries and performance footage, captures more than a few of those flashes...Way's voice is in top form, even when he's shrieking (because, seriously, even shrieking can be out of tune), and Life On The Murder Scene pulls all the right guns from My Chem's arsenal of songs. As live albums go, this one is A-O-f***ing-K."

The CD/DVD set was enthusiastically reviewed all over the place and fans embraced the package quickly. To thank their fans, MCR ran a contest on their Web site. If you preordered the set, you were entered to win a trip to Los Angeles to meet the band!

While the fervor built over *Life On The Murder Scene*, the band spent part of April tucked away at Eldorado Recording Studio in Burbank, California laying down tracks for their next record.

Chapter 10
tHe BlaCk PaRaDe

During the month of March it was time for the band to get down to work on their next studio album, *The Black Parade*. They selected producer Rob Cavallo (Green Day, Goo Goo Dolls, Michelle Branch, Alanis Morissette) to help them break through to the next level. Rob had the guys writing and demoing songs at the Paramour, a 70-year-old hilltop mansion in Silverlake, a posh Los Angeles neighborhood. The songs they worked on had been written and recorded on the band's tour bus in 2005. Early on in the process, Rob told MTV, "We're working on stuff, just getting it together and making demos. And from what we've got so far, I think the record is going to be awesome. The songs are wicked. There's some really dark stuff, and some touches of Queen and The Doors. And there's some really experimental parts that sound a bit like System Of A Down. But all of that is mixed with a big shot of My Chemical Romance."

Gerald told Mike Diver of *DrownedinSound.com* that the album was definitely a departure for the band: "There are strings and horns and a marching band on the new album. We got a big toy box, and got to do what we want. We got everything in our arsenal that we wanted, but luckily we've a sense about ourselves that stops us being self-indulgent, so we used just enough—well, that's what I feel. We went a little over the top, but never to the point of boring people."

"We've gotten to a point as a band where we feel we could stop holding back a little bit," Gerard admitted in the band's promotional video for *The Black Parade*. "It's a record that's so full of life, so risky, daring, fun. It makes you laugh; it makes you cry. 'Welcome To The Black Parade' is the one song that sums up the sound for the record, and all the risk we took jammed into one mini epic."

The record is actually conceptual in nature and follows one man, named "The Patient," through his illness and impending death. In a promotional video for the album, Gerard expounded on the theme, "'The Black Parade' is the very basic premise of the record, which is when you die, I'd like to think that death comes for you however you want. And I feel that it's your strongest memory, either from childhood or adulthood, and for this particular character in this record, his strongest memory is of being a child and his father is taking him to this parade. So when death comes for him, it comes in the form of a black parade."

To effectively sing from this character's point of view, Gerard went to some pretty drastic lengths, including cutting his hair short and bleaching it blond. He was wanted to take on the persona of someone going through this terrible illness and perhaps going through chemotherapy.

In a deep discussion with *Rolling Stone*, Gerard talked about his hopes for the new record. "There's just so much I want to say about real life now. We're starting to see the beauty of the world and to truly understand our relationships with other human beings like our loved ones," he said. "What's wrong with writing a song about missing somebody instead of vampire assassins? There's a common saying in My Chemical Romance that, 'This is bigger than us,' but what I've come to realize is that, at the same time, there's nothing bigger than the lives of the five guys in this band."
Truth be told, the band wanted the next record to be epic in proportion. "We all have

records that shaped our childhood and teen years," said Mikey. "When you hear a song, it shoots you back to a moment in time. We want this album to do that for people. We want the entire world to be moved." A lofty goal.

Gerard told Mike Diver of *DrownedinSound.com* that, "It's the record of our dreams. It's a record that you want to sit down with—you want to listen to the entire thing. Conceptually, I believe we've finally hit what we wanted—it's what we wanted to say."

The Black Parade is more than just the name of the album. It's the persona the entire band took on while working on the album. During the recording process, the band also kept up an impressive tour schedule.

On April 29, they headlined England's Give It A Name Festival at London's Earl Court. Other bands that played that night include Taint, The Honorary Title, Underoath, Thrice, The Ataris, and others.

In July, fans saw Gerard get back to his art roots with news that he would pen a comic book series for Dark Horse Comics dubbed *The Umbrella Academy*. According to Dark Horse there will be six issues in the series that focuses on Sir Reginald Hargreeves, a "world-renowned scientist and inventor, intrepid adventurer, successful entrepreneur, champion cricketer, and closet space alien. *Umbrella Academy* is the story of seven extraordinary, maladjusted individuals, their triumphs, tragedies, failures, and disappointments."

Spin boiled down the plot even more saying it was about kids needing to "learn to get past their spectacularly dysfunctional childhoods" to save the world. "When Gerard came to us, we were obviously excited and receptive to him doing comics," Jeremy Atkins of Dark Horse told *Spin*. "Once we saw it, we were totally sold." The series will be released in mid-2007 and eventually all six issues will be compiled into a graphic novel. Fans have already marked the event on their calendars.

While looking forward to new music and a comic book, San Diego fans were sadly disappointed when My Chem canceled a headline appearance on August 3 at the twenty-second annual Street Scene. Gerard and drummer Bob Bryar were both hurt during a video shoot for "Welcome To The Black Parade, the first single on their third studio album. Canceling was unavoidable since Gerard tore multiple ligaments in his ankle and Bob badly burned the back of his leg. (Sam Bayer was directing the video. He also worked on Nirvana's "Smells Like Teen Spirit" and all of Green Day's *American Idiot* videos.) After the event, rumors began to fly, so the band posted this message on their Web site:

"There are tons of rumors and allegations floating around, and we want to clear it up for all of you. Here are the facts and please know that none of the injuries sustained were permanent nor intentional. Last week, while shooting a new video for our new record...Gerard tore multiple ligaments in his ankle and Bob received a band burn to the back of his leg. These injuries were sustained on Thursday evening. On Friday morning, we drove to San Diego to prepare for our performance. After seeing doctors, we decided to give it our all and rehearse on Friday night. This provided impossible. The pain was overwhelming and we could not pull through without further injuring ourselves. So there you have it, there were no car wrecks, monster attacks, or alien abductions, but there were serious injuries that required this to be the way. We hate canceling shows, especially now that we are done recording and just want to play. We miss you all and will see you soon." —My Chemical Romance

A statement from the band's management to MTV underscored that information

saying, "The guys did all they could, including traveling to San Diego and attempting to rehearse against doctor's orders, however, when the injuries proved too painful to play, they decided not to push it any further. The band will return to San Diego in the near future, and they send their sincerest apologies to the fans that came out to see them."

The rest of August 2006 was a blur of concerts. On the 11th and 12th, My Chem returned to Japan to play the Summer Sonic Festival with Linkin Park, Metallica, Fall Out Boy, Tool, The Flaming Lips, and Massive Attack.

London's Hammersmith Palais welcomed back these most-favored punks on the 22nd with a sold-out show. But, the band had a surprise for their fans. When the lights went down and the band was to take the stage, an announcement was made: My Chemical Romance won't be able to make it to the show, but they sent The Black Parade in their place. There was some momentary confusion as some fans booed. But others seemed to have a clue as to what was really in store. As the lights went up, the kids knew the real score...here were the guys from My Chem getting into the character of The Black Parade. Fans were pumped hoping they'd hear some new music! According to Gerald, "We did it with full knowledge that when the announcement was being made, the kids would kind of know what the deal was. There was a little bit of theater to it, yeah. You listen to this new record, and there's that kind of ambition on it-it's the ambition of hopefully bringing rock to that place where it's majestic again, where it's theatrical again. There's a pageantry to rock that's been missing, and that's the ambition on the new record." The band played some new material, as well as "I'm Not Okay," "Ghost Of You," "Cemetery Drive," and "Helena."

The band also played the NextFestival on the 6th at Red Rocks Amphitheatre in Colorado. Also playing on the bill were the All-American Rejects, Rosehill Drive, and Head Click.

On the 24th while My Chem opened for Muse in Edinburgh, Scotland, fans everywhere celebrated their Best Band On The Planet tip of the hat from the *Kerrang!* Awards. My Chem hit the main stage at the Reading Festival on the 27th but were surprised when fans started throwing trash at them onstage! It's unclear if the crowd was merely rowdy or if they were actually dissing the band.

> **"There's a pageantry to rock that's been missing, and that's the ambition on the new record."**
> **-Gerard**

Fans finally got the chance to hear My Chem's latest single, "Welcome To The Black Parade," when the band played it live on August 28 at MTV's *Red Carpet On The Rock*, the Video Music Awards preshow. The single hit radio in mid-September and on September 6, a few lucky fans paid just two bucks to see My Chem at the Trocadero Theatre in Philadelphia. The show was recorded for MTV's *$2 Bill* series. Labor Day weekend brought a few stateside shows including Allentown, Pennsvylvania on the 2nd and Syracuse, New York on the 3rd.

By October, anticipation among MCR fans reached a fevered pitch. The new record—*The Black Parade*—was only days away from being released on October 24. (U.K. fans were able to buy the album a day earlier.) As of press time, the tracks on the record included "The End" / "Dead" / "Disappear" / "A Kiss Before She Goes" / "Welcome To The Black Parade" / "I Don't Love You" / "House Of Wolves" / "Cancer" / "Momma" / "Sleep" / "Teenagers" / "Disenchanted" / "Famous Last Words"

Guitarist Frank Iero happily discussed the album with *Metal Hammer* saying, "[Producer] Rob [Cavallo] was integral to this project. He has such a pure love of music that it becomes infectious. He can talk about music in terms of emotions, and help you convey those emotions in the correct way." Ray Toro agreed saying, "Sonically, Rob is a master. It is a joy to watch him craft tones that make your song sound like you always dreamed it would."

Gerard told AOL Music that the album "is way more dramatic, way more theatrical, completely over the top, borderline psychotic. It's the most pure, intense thing we've ever been involved in. We just didn't mess around at all. To be honest with you, it felt like we did at the beginning when we did [our first record], that's the kind of intensity that we got." On a conceptual level, the album focuses on a character cryptically called "the Patient."

"It's been the experience of our dreams," Gerard went on to tell AOL. "It felt like we got to reinvent the wheel for ourselves. We weren't afraid to do anything."

When asked if the record had commercial appeal, Gerald told *DrownedinSound.com*, "I don't think it's ever a conscious decision to write mainstream songs. In fact, I think some of the structure is the opposite of mainstream structure, but the idea was to directly affect people in a larger way, in a more direct way. That was the objective with this record—we wanted to cross over to many people, so that this affects lives, lots of lives."

In late August 2006, My Chem launched a Web site specifically for their new studio album at *www.theblackparade.com*. Fans got the first glimpse of a change in the way the band looks. Gerard sports a new, very short haircut and his gorgeous black hair has been bleached blond! Mikey's given up his glasses and darkened his hair in counterpoint to his brother's new golden locks. The rest of the band is also experimenting with new do's. Other stylistic changes include their logo, which now resembles the typeface used on the cover of *The Black Parade*.

The month of October closed out with an appearance at the eighth annual Voodoo Music Experience in New Orleans' City Park on October 28 to 30. Headliners were Red Hot Chili Peppers and Duran Duran. Supporting bands included MCR, Wu- Tang Clan, Flaming Lips, and Kings Of Leon, to name a few.

Despite rave reviews for the new record, My Chem will always be best known as a kick-ass live band. The guys love playing for their fans and living off the energy of the kids moshing down front. Ray Toro told Joanna Davila of *University Wire* that, "We play with passion and energy and we love what we do; we wouldn't want to be doing anything else."

In an interview with *Rolling Stone's* Jenny Eliscu, Gerard demystified My Chem's onstage theatrics, "You see us playing these songs about fictitious gunfights, cowboys, electric chairs, and getting f***ed in jail. The abstraction is there for a reason. It's for people to get what they want out of it. This band is therapy for us. What we're saying through the performance is, 'This can or cannot be therapy for you too. Either way, we'll still do it.'"

Perhaps Gerard best summed it up for the *Alternative Press*: "For me, [being onstage] is me being everything I always wanted to be. It erases everything I hate about myself. Nothing can hurt me. I feel completely invincible. I feel like everyone else on that stage is invincible and we're capable of anything. There's no stopping us."

U.S. DiscOgraPhy

SiNGLES

"I'm Not Okay (I Promise)"
"Helena"
"The Ghost Of You"

ALBUMS

The Black Parade
The End / Dead / Disappear / A Kiss
Before She Goes / Welcome To The
Black Parade / I Don't Love You /
House Of Wolves / Cancer / Momma /
Sleep / Teenagers / Disenchanted /
Famous Last Words
October 24, 2006 / Reprise

Three Cheers For Sweet Revenge
Helena / Give 'Em Hell, Kid / To The
End / You Know What They Do To
Guys Like Us In Prison / I'm Not Okay
(I Promise) / The Ghost Of You / The
Jetset Life Is Gonna Kill You / Interlude
/ Thank You For The Venom / Hang 'Em
High / It's Not A Fashion Statement, It's
A Deathwish / Cemetery Drive / I
Never Told You What I Do For A Living
June 8, 2004 / Reprise

I Brought You My Bullets, You Brought Me Your Love
Honey, This Mirror Isn't Big Enough
For The Two Of Us / Vampires Will
Never Hurt You / Drowning Lessons /
Our Lady Of Sorrows / Headfirst For
Halos / Skylines And Turnstiles / Early
Sunsets Over Monroeville / This Is The
Best Day Ever/ Cubicles / Demolition
Lovers / Vampires Will Never Hurt You
(bonus video) / Honey This Mirror
Isn't Big Enough For The Two Of Us
(bonus video)
July 23, 2002 / Eyeball Records

COMPiLATiONS / GREATEST HiTS

Life On The Murder Scene
Audio CD: Thank You For The Venom /
Cemetery Drive / Give 'Em Hell, Kid /
Headfirst For Halos / Helena / You
Know What They Do To Guys Like Us
In Prison / Ghost Of You / I'm Not Okay
(I Promise) / I Never Told You What I
Do For A Living (demo) / Bury Me In
Black (demo) / Desert Song (demo)
DVD: I'm Not Okay (I Promise) /
Cemetery Drive / Our Lady Of Sorrows
/ Honey, This Mirror Isn't Big Enough
For The Two Of Us / You Know What
They Do To Guys Like Us In Prison /
Headfirst For Halos / Ghost Of You /
Thank You For The Venom / Give 'Em
Hell, Kid / Vampires Will Never Hurt
You / Helena
March 21, 2006 / Reprise

Underworld: Evolution
"To The End"
January 10, 2006 / Lakeshore Records

Tony Hawk's American Wasteland
"Astro Zombies"
October 18, 2005 / Vagrant Records

*House of Wax: Music From the
Motion Picture*
"I Never Told You What I Do For A
Living"
May 3, 2005 / Maverick

Nintendo Fusion Tour Music Sampler

In Honor: A Compilation To Beat Cancer
"Headfirst For Halos" (live)
September 21, 2004 / Vagrant Records

ViDEOS / DVDs

See Life On The Murder Scene *in the*
"Compilations / Greatest Hits" category.